1124

India Epps

PALMETTO PUBLISHING
Charleston, SC
www.PalmettoPublishing.com

1124

First Edition

Paperback ISBN: 978-1-68515-835-4

1124

I dedicate this book to Chayce. Your big brother not only named you, but he loved you as if you were his son. The bond the two of you share as brothers will forever carry you, and he will forever live thru you. Always remember, the soul never dies, Truiee is forever with you Chayce.

I'm heartbroken forever. There's no such thing as closure when you lose a child to murder.

Love you both immensely,
Forever Mommy

Table of Contents

"EVERY MORNING I WAKE UP WITH A POSITIVE MINDSET TO GO GET IT, EVEN IF I FAIL I ALWAYS THINK WITH A POSITIVE MINDSET TO STAY STRONG."

TRUIEE

Chapter 1

I'm Sorry

Sunday **November 24, 2019**, four days before Thanksgiving, the sun had went down and a dark cloud covered the city. The sound of cars riding by faded out by gunshots. A little after 6 pm, everything changed. Gunshots rang out on Greenmount avenue. (Bow, Bow, Bow, Bow, Bow, Bow , Boom, Boom, Boom). Inside the convenience store, he layed there fighting for his life, taking his last breath of air.

> "Blood coming down my face , I can't see out of my eyes,
> I can hear the ambulance as I heard my mother cry.
> Body aching from the pain, feel I'm bout to die.
> The Lord asked me was I ready?,
> I responded why.
> The paramedics asked my name but I could not reply.
> Who at the hospital to meet me, it's homicide."

I get a text saying my son was shot!! Oh My God!! Nooooooo!!!I immediately rush to the Emergency Room at Johns Hopkins Hospital. Frantic, heart beating fast, voice shaking, as my body tremble as I say my son name.

Please somebody help me, my son! My son! I stand at the desk as my body is weak, my stomach wouldn't stop balling up in knots as a eerie feeling that I've never felt before take over my body. I began to bang my hand on the desk as I ask to get to the back to see my son. Is he ok?! Is he alive?! Is my son ok!! The look on the receptionist face said it all. She was speechless but her face spoke volumes of pain. She told me to go to the back and wait for the doctor to come out and talk to me. As she pressed the button for me to enter the back, tears drip from my face, as I hurry to the back room. I began to pace the floor back and forth, back and forth, waiting for the doctor. The wait grew longer, and longer, and I continued to scream where is my son?! What room is he in?!, through the entire waiting area. My body was going through changes. My soul was crying!! My heart racing, eyes bloodshot red from crying. After screaming so loud I became dehydrated.

A tall white man with a long white Doctor's coat entered the room, he was looking down as he spoke, something just didn't feel right when he came in the room. When he spoke, it sounded like he was talking in slow motion. All I remembered him saying was, "I'm Sorry Mam, but your son didn't make it." My eyes closed and I lost my mind. A scream from the pit of my stomach and soul cried out in a scream of a mother's pain. They shut the door and removed my youngest son from out of the room with me. I lost it!! Noooooooooooooo!!! I blacked out, the room got dark, I kicked, I screamed I tried to rip the room apart. I opened the door and screamed "where is he"?" I need to see him now!" Security escorted me down a long hallway. This has to be a lie! My son has to be in one of these rooms waiting for me. They must have made a mistake! Either way, they must have the wrong person. Where is my child?

I turn to the right. There he is behind a glass, laying in the hospital bed with covers on as if he is sleeping! They have his mouth propped open. Oh my God, it's really my son!!! I bang on the glass, and scream Mommy loves you! I can't believe my eyes. I try to bust through the police to get into the room my son was laying in, but the door was locked. Twisting and turning a door-knob that won't turn. Crying, Screaming telling my son to "wake up!"" Get up Tionne!!" I know he heard me, but he couldn't move, there he lay, lifeless, unable to take another breath. I moaned my pain and his name for as long as they allowed me back there. As they tried to remove me, I grabbed the glass. Holding on to the window as I scream my child's name. Tionnneeeeeeeee!!! His name fading away with my cry as I scream for my son to wake up and come on.

How can the child I carried for 9 months and raised for 22 years, how is it they he lay in the hospital bed, lifeless, and I'm restricted from touching my son. I'm told he was a crime scene and I'm not allowed in the room with him! What?!! What?!! This is my child. I birthed him! This is my son! My youngest son stroked his hand down my back and whispered, "it's ok Ma, he hears you." "Tionne hears you Ma". Here it is my youngest son had to hold me as we cry together watching my oldest son shot, 4 times in the upper body, one bullet traveled and hit his heart. "How?!"

"Why, my child?" "I'm Sorry Son!" "I'm Sorry this happened to you!!" So many questions, no answers.

The worst pain a mother could ever endure is to see their child murdered! Laying there and there's nothing I could do to save him.

My Firstborn Son,
First One I Birthed,
First One I Raised,
And First One I Buried.

My heart and soul is broken forever. I can't even process the fact that this is real, I'm in denial, I don't wanna believe this is happening. I'm angry, I'm Hurt, Mad, Sad, Disgusted, Heartbroken, Confused, my soul is crying. A part of me is forever missing.

I ride to the scene after leaving the emergency room, just to cry and pray in the exact spot where my son was murdered. Pain I can barely describe in words.

I can't sleep, I'm pacing my bedroom, my head pounding with nonstop headaches from crying, screaming, and yelling. I'm empty. I feel lifeless. I'm here, but I'm not. Up all night crying and thinking. Praying and crying. Crying and pacing the floor.

The sun comes up moments after pacing all night. As I gaze out the front door, a red cardinal bird lands on my porch. I stare at the bird as a tear forms in my eyes, and slowly my tears fill my face as I watch this bird land and sit for minutes on my porch. As God was already sending me a sign that Tionne was ok, and although I didn't wanna accept the fact that my son was just murdered, I still had to thank God for the signs that was brought before my eyes even in the midst of losing my child.

I prayed and asked my son to tell me what happened and slowly but surely, I began to understand the signs.

I went straight to the scene bright and early. The streets talk, and I needed to hear everything they was saying. My heart racing, I can't believe this is where my son took his last breath. Rage fill my body as I approach the scene. I walk down the street from where it actually happened to listen at people on the bus stop. I hear people talking, whispering that it was a shooting yesterday and a kid got killed. I remained silent so I could hear what they had to say without them knowing who I was, or noticing that I wasn't really catching the bus. It was pain running through my body as even the words were being spoken around me. I sat and acted as if I was waiting on the bus just to blend in with the surroundings. Some people expressed their concerns over the killings repeatedly in the city, others spoke what they were hearing from news to hear say. I sat and took it all in and just listened to see what I could gather from down the street from where the murder took place. As the crowd on the bus stop scattered, I walked up the street, somebody knows something, somebody had to see something yesterday. I canvassed the store where he was murdered and noticed a camera facing the entry way. I looked across the street and noticed a camera at the apartment building. A white truck pulled up, look like a working man inside. I saw him talking to a lady so I asked him if he had heard about the boy who got shot yesterday. He spoke of how nice the kid was and mentioned a lady house that he knew of that would be familiar to the kid. When I asked where, he pointed to an apartment building. As I entered the apartment building I began to knock on all the apartment doors. When I reached the last apartment, a bald lady answered and looked kind of skeptical to talk to me.

My heart started beating real fast, my adrenaline began to rush like something was wrong. As she tried to close the door on me, I placed my foot in the doorway to stop her. I asked if she knew my son and showed her a picture of him. The look she had on her face was speechless. She held her head down and replied, Yes.

I started to welcome myself in her house to look around, and noticed my son's tennis shoes. It was like he led me right to her. She started talking and trying to explain that his brother had just left there on the night of the murder, right after my son was shot and killed. When she described who and said his name, I knew exactly who she was referring to. The look on her face was shocking, but she look like she really wanted me to know every-thing she knew. She started to explain the evening of 1124.

"Some shit that's understood can't be explained,
and lately I been going through some things, Feel
The Fire In My Soul."
"Sorry, Sorry, Sorry, Sorry, Sorry, Sorry, Sorry,
Sor-ry,
Streets made me Heartless, Heartless, Heartless,
Heartless, Heartless, Heartless, Heartless,
Heart-le-ss
Yea, Yea, Yea

Truiee

"BULLETS RIP YOUR TISSUE HAVE YOU LEAKING, GOT YOUR HOMIE TWEAKING, WHY YOU LEAVE YOUR BROTHER ON THE CEMENT, WATCH HIM HAVING TROUBLE WITH HIS BREATHING. DIE FOR NO REASON, NIGGAS BE DYING FOR NO REASON."

TRUIEE

Chapter 2

My Decisions

The streets was talking. All I knew for sure was my son was with his brother and his cousin on his dad side, and my son was the only one murdered. He wasn't the only one shot, but he was the only one dead. Flashbacks of the hospital played in the back of my mind. I didn't see any blood on his brother, so how is it that he held him until paramedics got there, with not a trace of blood on him? An unidentified male was all I knew that waited for police to arrive. His wallet, bankcard, phone, all of his belongings were stolen. Something wasn't adding up, but I was determined to get to the bottom of what happened to my child on 1124.

Baltimore a cold hearted city, located in Maryland. A city full of jealousy, envy, betrayal, pain runs deep in this city. Lots of hidden talent that was being suffocated by murder. A lot of money made in Baltimore, it was the city with the main biggest port for production, known as The Port of Baltimore. A lot of drugs was brought in thru the Port. The Rich get Rich off of our city, and the poor die trying. It's like a goldmine covered with crime. Life and death was losing its value by the number. It was more homicides than high school graduates and that was a statistic. The city was grimy. More crime committed by people you knew, than a stranger.

I put my baby through private school at an early age. From the age of seven (7) years old, he was writing raps. From an early age my son had a passion for music. I would search his bookbag for homework every day and find the beginning of what would one day turn out to be his legacy.

The son of a hustler, yet fatherless, but raised by a single mother. His father was a seasoned veteran in the game. He was known to be from the east-side of the city. He based his life and reputation in the streets on loyalty, however his life was still impacted by his surroundings. He caught a bid of seven years, and to me that was a chance for me to take my son out of Baltimore for a change and chance for a better upbringing.

We moved down South. Atlanta became our new home for the next five (5) years. Truiee was around celebrities at an early age. Our first apartment in Atlanta was shared with my sister, at the time she was cool with the guy from the rap group "Young Gunz", and so Truiee was introduced to people in the music industry ever since he was a little boy. My sister Kelli was his favorite aunt, so everything about her to him was special.

Truiee smile would light up a room as soon as he entered it. His energy and personality was so pleasing to be around. He had his father's brown complexion and slanted eyes, his father's pointy nose, with his mother's smile and wisdom and kindness.

He was the perfect mixture of his parents, as his favorite aunt on his dad side would say. He brought out the best of both of us. He loved anything where you had to truly think and analyze. He was amazing with wires. He could fix anything electrical just by looking at it and thinking. He loved music. He would make a song that had true meaning and as you listen, the song would paint a picture and share a story.

Tionne had a positive mindset. He had a gift he was born with from God, which allowed him to be well connected with his spirit. He could see things before they happen and put it in a form of a story. It's like he had been here before. He learned self-manifestation at an early age. He knew his gift. He was motivation in human form himself. He was the voice! He would inspire all those around him and he stood out no matter where he was. There was a light that shined from within him, and it's like it was contagious. You could feel his energy and motivation. His wisdom and energy alone would drive you to Push Harder! Dream Bigger! Plan Wisely and Keep Your Faith No Matter the Situation and Keep Going. He was a loving person and fun to be around. His friends called him, "The Life of The Party".

My Firstborn Son and only child by me until he turned 11 years old, and I birthed another child.

He was the youngest boy on his father side. His brother on his dad side was older than him. They had a strange relationship. Truiee loved his older brother, but just like the story in the bible of "Cane and Abel", his brother envied him deep down inside. It's almost like his brother on his father side had a love/ hate type of bond. It's like he loved and envied my son. My son knew his brother was greedy at heart and possessed a jealous spirit, however his love for him never changed.

"YOU GONNA MEET A GREEDY
ASS PERSON ONE DAY. DON'T BE
OUT HERE, YOU KNOW CARRYING
A WHOLE BUNCH OF BAD VIBES ,
AND ENERGY ON YOUR SHOULDER.
YOU CAN NATURALLY FEEL IF A
PERSON AIN'T RIGHT, OR IF YOU
GOTTA FUNNY FEELING ABOUT
SOMEONE'S VIBES."

Truiee

At the age of 12 we Moved back to Baltimore. Truiee missed his family and friends so it took no time for him to adjust back to the city life. Although he was different, the life his mother never wanted for him calls him. After graduation I was so proud of him. He had completed a very important milestone in life, graduating from high school.

Working at U.P.S. I couldn't be happier for my baby to see him growing and taking his music to the next level. Endless temptations, all hell breaks loose.

Although he was the type to stay out of the way, the missing links from him yearning to have a bond with his father grew farther apart. The pain that cut deep within him never goes away. Relationship becomes cold, and their family tradition sucks him in so deep that he falls victim to the game. He started to hang around his father side heavy. The insatiable addiction to music and money had him around the wrong family members. Although they teased him about his dreams and laughed at his positive messages, he still tried to lead by example and push them to be a better version of themselves. He saw more in them than they saw in themselves. And although he stayed off the radar, he still loved his family no matter their wrongdoings.

"Related by blood but that don't mean our family good, they kept telling lies I had to cut some family ties, that bitch is a dog so I can show that hoe no forgiveness."

Truiee

The streets of Baltimore came with a great sacrifice called Life. You could pay the price for someone else just by being at the wrong place at the wrong time.

"I can't get caught lacking with my head down,
Gotta keep your head high,
Through the hard times and the dark pounds, I
got family fighting cases right now.
I be feeling lonely, I know niggas that will kill
their homies, so I can' t be surrounded by no
phonies.
Niggas play the 50, why you say you riding
You ain't with me.
Got me thinking, you plotting how to get me."

Truiee

Chapter 3

Testify

His cousin was in somebody paperwork, and in my city, that never ended good.

> "These niggas testify, so they don't go down by
> they self,
> My mind set on the riches
> I think rapping my way out.
> I started up, I keep flipping and breaking
> everything down. I can't afford to take no 'L" so
> I'm cutting off all my rounds."

Truiee

Truiee wrote true stories. Many of the stories were about his surroundings or people's lives that he was around. His music was his connection to the world. It showed what life was like to grow up in Baltimore through Truiee's eyes. Truiee knew his music was real, raw, and personal. He broke down the street code and how to be different no matter your surroundings. He used his wisdom to show young people his age and show his peers how to overcome the struggle of survival by education. Politics was one of his favorite topics to speak on. He would enlighten people on the hidden gems that was covered up by politicians so that people just like him, young black men knew they were more powerful in a suit and tie being educated than the lies that were told to black men to keep them suppressed and victims of the system. He was well rounded from street knowledge, to book smart. He was known jokingly as the hood preacher. He made it cool to be smart, and have swag and style. Having knowledge is power, and in Baltimore, the more you knew, the more dangerous you were to waking up your community to change, and learning a better way.

**"Loyalty is a must,
They was in it together its either death before
dishonor now that niggas a goner. "**

Truiee knew the streets was talking about his peeps and he also knew that what his cousin did was wrong so he kept his distance. He knew he didn't wanna be associated with a person who was putting other people lives in danger just to keep themselves free from the consequences. Everyone knew who was involved, but where I'm from everybody mind their business.

"My city wicked
All these niggas just some bitches who telling,
Stick to the code,
Never fold,
And get back to the cheddar.
Rain, Snow, Sleet, Sun,
We gon trap any weather"

Truiee

A city known as crabs in a barrel. Nobody wanted to see nobody get ahead. It wasn't the streets that didn't play fair, it was people in the streets cheating to win and doing anything to anybody to get ahead. Even your own family.

Truiee was on the rise to success, but in between jobs he hustled to flip his money and put back into his music. He had a plan. I always taught him if he fail to plan than plan to fail. At the same time he loved his family, and loving them from a distance sometimes still ended him back in their circle. And although he wasn't a main target, his loyalty to his family cost the price of his LIFE!.

" His simple ass lied to me when he could have
been honest.
You gotta keep your composure,
And get all your shit together,
He pillow talking to bitches,
And then gone fold under pressure."

Truiee

THEY SEEN THE FIRE IN MY EYES AND TRY TO WATER ME DOWN

Truiee

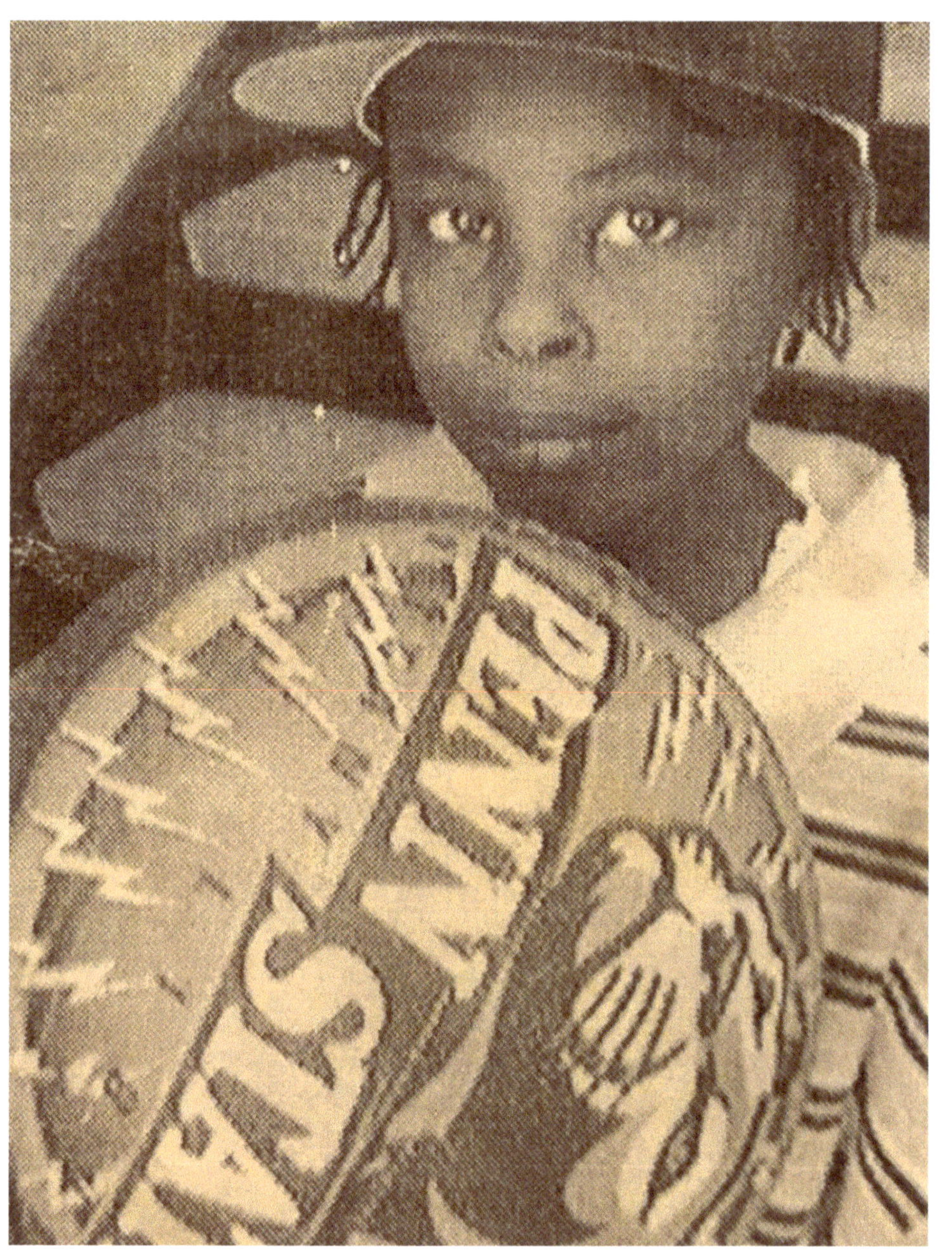

Chapter 4

Fire In Me

I heard they watch me cuz I'm cocky so they
copy my style,
They asking questions what you call yourself
foxing me out,
I roll with the beef
you niggas ain't goin slaughter me now.
They seen the fire in my eyes and try to water me down.

Truiee

Truiee was spoiled rotten. Between me and his grandmother's, My Dear, he didn't want for anything. Truiee was different. He was laid back but you could see the spark in his eyes. His spirit and his energy told it all. He wanted everybody to win. No matter where he was at he was always encouraging and giving people the key to life. That beef had nothing to do with him. Absolutely nothing!

Truiee just wanted to make it out the struggle with his music. Truiee had never been in trouble until he started being around them. His loyalty and love for his family became deadly.

1124 Truiee was brutally murdered. His face flash all over the news. The newspaper stands in black and white print headlines, 22 year old Baltimore Local Artist, Tionne Jones, murdered on 1124. But see my son already knew how they were. Deep down my son was positive and told them motivating ways to mani-fest their dreams. My son knew who he was, and had a positive impact on anybody he came in contact with. But the betrayal and selfish ways of his family began to poison him. Their fake love began to draw him in. And even though he knew they wasn't right, he still was loyal and had love for his family.

"I follow my spirit it show me all my strengths
where I'm gifted,
A mind of a genius,
The system labeled me as a menace.
I open my eyes and manifested all of my wishes,
I told 'em the secret, them niggas laughed at me
like I'm senseless."

Truiee

See the whole time they was laughing in his face, they didn't real-ize he was so in tune with his spirit, he spoke truth before it even happened. While they laughing in his face about his messages, his inspiration, his positive outpouring, he was writing rap lyrics about them the whole time. Making albums, making history. No matter their cruddy ways, he continued to be him and really left a positive impact on the world with the fact that he was differ- ent. His music told his story. As I listened he told me the whole murder. Through his music, bits and pieces from each song. His music tells me what happened on 1124.

**"I been in the streets,
You niggas just wanna be in the mix.
I showed you the way,
We pose to be like Lilo and Stitch,
I kept shit real, you pose to kept your mouth silent.
I stand on my own,
I stood up for my family wrongs,
The Last of my breed, but Ima make us multiply strong."**

Truiee

Truiee knew his family seen the fire in his eyes. They knew he was gonna make it with his music. They knew his messages was up- lifting, but they was non-believers. Non-believers of karma. See karma comes back no matter what, she will spin the block quick.

They knew Truiee was a genius for real. He was before his time. He would speak knowledge to your soul. He led you to a higher level in life. He often went to sleep at night listening to podcast and daily affirmations that were soothing to the soul. He was the same no matter who he was around.

**"A lot of niggas lose they self, and forget who
they are,
Because of the niggas that they hang around.
Always remember yo,
Keep your same personality yo, don't never
change your character, Just stay 100 man."**

Truiee

Truiee was loved in every hood, every part of the city. East, West, North, and South. He stood out. He was different. He was a leader and wasn't afraid to stand on his beliefs. He never agreed to being cruddy to nobody.

**"They seen the fire in my eyes and try to water
me down."**

Truiee knew he would one day be a LeGend. It was in him. See you can't practice character. Your character speaks volumes of who you are. Now you can practice behavior, but not character. And Truiee's character spoke for himself. He was true to the world, and the world likes to be lied to. But the world respected him for the light that he brought that would change and uplift you without you even putting forth effort. Because his words was powerful, and his spirit was in tune with his purpose. He knew who he was, and he poured wisdom into dark places.

And although he was related to some cruddy people, his name wasn't Truiee for no reason. He was true to his self. He was true to others. His messages was to influence you to not be a victim of your surroundings. To think Big Be Big. To Dream Bigger than what's in front of you. Most important without God, nothing was possible!

Truiee had a certain aura about himself. He brought peace when his spirit was around. He was funny and loved to joke. Everybody loved Tionne. He was just that type of guy.

I found a message in my son phone, where he sent to his cousin, that he knew his purpose in life, and his cousin responded, "u funny." And that same cousin that ridiculed him being positive about his life, and purpose of being, and his wisdom, was the same reason he was killed.

Jealousy starts from love. And the fake love caused his death.

Seven is the number of completion, the seven titles of his songs on his last album, are the seven chapters of this book. The seven chapters of His Life and Death.

On 1124 his life changed. His life went on to a higher form called death. From the signs he sent me, to the information homicide gave me when he was killed, it all matched. His music was the voice I needed to tell me What happened on 1124. Who murdered my son? Why would this happen to my child? All my questions, all my answers, right in front of me. See what's done in the dark, ALWAYS COMES TO LIGHT.

A lot of niggas out here lose they self
and forget who they are ,

Because of the niggas that they hang
around..

Always remember , keep your same
personality .

Don't never change your character,
just stay 100 man

Chapter 5

Risk

"Now I'm thinking to myself , I can't get caught
up at the light, I guess they tryna take me out, or
they tryna pull me down. They don't want Truiee
to smile they just want Tionne to frown so I gotta
keep my head above the water."

Truiee

Truiee music was his dream, but his passion was to touch
lives. No matter what obstacles he faced, he remained
humble. As any young person he didn't always make the right
decisions in life, however he knew the risks. Trying to be positive and uplift your community and your culture came with a big
price. In his mind, he wasn't doing it for him. Everything he did
was to one day be able to give his family the world, especially his

baby brother Chayce. He didn't have any children of his own, so his baby brother was the closest to him.

Back and forth in the studio with his best friend Ant, they had always promised each other that one day they would make it. From the basement since they were kids making music, to the stage making history. But Truiee was torn in between following his dreams and still spending time with his other side of his family, looking for love from his father that he didn't get. I would always tell my son to be careful around them. The more I tried to keep him from the fake love, it was like the more he gravitated to them. He knew the vicious cycle they were breeding, and it would lead to destruction, it was just a matter of time. His loyalty to those he loved was unmatched, however loyalty ended up in murder.

"I be on the mount where it's green, and they know L&B is where I claim, I ain't never gon change."

Truiee

Truiee was mindful of his surroundings, but eventually his decision to team up with his other side of his family lead to the risk of a dangerous lifestyle. He started hustling with his other side of the family, which was against my wishes, however it's like they weren't satisfied until they could get him involved with their lifestyle. That led to him being arrested. I always spoke life into my son and continued to remind him of positive affirmations, which he spoke daily on his social media platform. Although I warned him constantly of the bad influence, they displayed, he chose to name himself just that, Mr. Bad Influence. But despite being called Mr. bad Influence, he actually was the exact opposite. He instead, was a positive influence despite his mistakes. He would make videos daily giving inspiration and motivating messages to inspire people to keep going and find your gift. No matter what family you were born into, it was up to you to be accountable for your journey. He spoke about being mindful of the closest ones too you, and how jealousy started from love.

His music was so true, that it actually in the end told his story as well. Tionne was a lyrical genius. He would write a song and have you feeling as if you were there. His music would tell a story. Being different, in His eyes, was his only option.

Endless temptations led to run in with the law and arrest. Truiee had been assaulted by police at our house, probation, and now fighting a charge, Truiee was in between a gift and a curse. A gift of knowing his purpose and leaving an impact that would turn into his legacy, and a curse of being betrayed and killed by a family member.

No matter which way he turned he faced risk. Risk of snakes, risk of jail, risk of police brutality, risk of betrayal, risk of death.

No matter the risk, Truiee Praise and Faith was greater than his pain. His impact was louder than his risk, and his life was lived with purpose. His mistakes turned into lessons, and his enemies could never block his blessings, because his spirit, God never rejected.

"It's the Risk that you take nigga,
Gotta watch out for these fake niggas,
Middle finger to the jakes nigga,

Watch out for these snakes nigga.
It's the risk that you take nigga,
It's the risk that you take."

Truiee

Chapter 6

STRANGE FRUIT

"Look my brother why we killing each other,
They want us to hate and get rid of each other
It's in our face, but we color blind,
The fact's they giving us is all a lie.
The Higher Power is the Black opp
A real gangster ain't a bad guy,
He's a black man with a suit and tie,
They will kill Obama if he reveal his secret, but
instead he push us to be better people.
We are still in slavery, we have no freedom, but
there's still a chance, we are not defeated, to
gain all the power we must be conceded.
You should've listened to your father,
now you a problem solver,
gotta stay wit your revolver.

Bodies you keep white chalkin,
Thought you was getting married,
Bitch I left you at the altar.
People love to see me down.
I can see it through these clowns,
It's different vibes when I'm round,
Hating on me cause my sound.
Why you wanna take my crown?
Put me six in the ground,
And my right-hand man, just had told me how he felt
I'm in this shit all by myself.
My cousins actin all phony,
My brother put his hands on me,
Ion want your love homey.
I do better by my lonely.
Ion fuck wit my father,
He don't fuck wit me,
It is what it really is
Ion care what it be
We would never be the same
He called his own son lame
Now washed-up old man.
He flashed money in my face,
In front a whole bunch of snakes
I walked off on his ass
He thought he put me in my place
They laughing all in each other's face.
He loss all my respect
And I would never give it back

He used A.I. for a check
But I ain't have to tell you that."

Truiee

The world was his canvas, and music was his expression of how he saw the world around him. How the closest people too you, were the ones you had to watch the most.

Tionne grew up with an old soul. His mind was very inquisitive, and he was beyond his time. He was raised around a lot of wisdom. His great grandmother, grandma India, pretty much raised him along with mother, and grandmother who he loved so much, My Dear. Tionne was different, a deep thinker. Tionne carried a positive energy within him. You felt his energy and it uplifted you or made you smile when he was around. He was a vibe.

He had a passion for History. He used politics in his lyrics to spread messages of the truth that was hidden from blacks.

Being mistreated by family, he began to realize, he stood alone.

He always knew he was different. Tionne made a song called STRANGE FRUIT, remade after Billie Holiday. When he explained what it was, it was deep. Strange Fruit was a representation of the blood that was shed from our ancestors being hung on trees and lynched, and the leaves would turn colors from the blood, which back then was known as a term called strange fruit.

He would rap about the things that triggered his feelings towards his family, the truth behind it all.

He wrote songs to remind us that no matter what we were stripped of, that our minds could never be taken.

He spoke of broken relationships between him and his father. His hurt superseded his love, and his love spoke his pain. Tionne knew he was great. He knew his gift. Tionne knew things before it even happened. He was blessed with the gift of dreaming. He would dream things before they even happened, and then rap about it in a story. He was a Dreamer, and music was Tionne gateway to his Dreams. He was music, and his music was messages. He drew your soul in with his lyrics. There was power in his gift. But with Power comes Pain.

His Plan was to Push thru the Pain to Persevere, to Progress, and then Manifest his gift. Who would ever think it would end with Death?! But see Death was just the **physical ending**, but his **Spiritual Beginning**. On **1124 Tionne died, but Truiee Became A LEGEND.**

Chapter 7

No Reason

I woke up crying, breathing real hard, panting deep breaths! It was the most real dream I ever had in my life. He was right there. My son! My son was talking too me! He told me everything! He took me on a ride. He took me to the store and showed me the entire murder, where and how it took place. He told me that he couldn't get out of the store when they was shooting. He told me it wasn't for him and he was sorry he had to leave me. He told me to listen to his music, he would tell me everything. I couldn't stop crying. I went to grab him and hug him and he disappeared. I woke up crying, hugging myself, as if I had reached, and no one was there. How miraculous that he came to me in a dream.

Then I thought back to his best friend coming to me, right after my son was murdered, and said he dreamed my son was standing in the closet. He couldn't understand what my son was trying to tell him. But there was something about a lady, and a closet. I had to pay attention to the SIGNS. The murder is right in front of me. He was talking to us through Dreams. He told me his entire murder through dreams and his music. The Lady in his best friend dream, was in reality the lady that would tell me pieces to the murder. The closet, was the closet where his belongings were stashed by his brother, after he robbed my son instead of calling the ambulance and waiting with him for help. He was a Dreamer and he sent all his signs in Dreams.

**"Every morning I wake up with a positive mindset
to go get it,
Even if I fail, I always think with a positive
mindset to stay strong."**

Truiee

Truiee left a positive impact on everybody, which is the key to being a LeGend. Not about who you are. But the biggest thing about life is what type of impact you leave behind to inspire someone else to be great.

Tionne, who would soon evolve into Truiee, understood Legacy at an early age. A couple days before his murder, he made a video that he never even had a chance to see it once it was complete, because he was murdered, right after he made the video. I felt like that was his last message.

**"It's been a cold ass day"
"I been in a long hallway"
"I know they wanna real, real me"**

"I can't go nowhere"
"I been through the storm, no rain"
"Hopefully you feel my pain"
"Don't leave me baby"
"I'm hoping you believe me baby"
"Them niggas wanna be me baby"
"You forever my Lady"

Truiee

It's like I started to not just listen but hear his messages, his knowledge, his gems, all hidden in his gift, his music. The sound of the beat was all in tune with his story. I'm forever his lady.

Truiee music told his story. It's like the book being told by me and Truiee. Don't just listen to his music, listen to his message. His story makes up the word history. Truiee story will forever be a part of history.

Truiee died for no reason, but his legacy lives on forever. You will forever hear his voice through his music. His loyalty outweighed the hate around him.

The cousin on his father side that was telling on a nigga years ago. Well you know what they say, eventually the person you told on, comes home one day, and Truiee was at the wrong place at the wrong time.

Crazy thing is one of the cruddy buddies that was paid and sent to take the cousin out, was actually related to Truiee. So not only was he killed because of someone shooting at his family member, he was also killed by a family member.

Karma, the only thing that never miss. 90 days later both shooters that shot my son was dead. Cruddy buddies had been cruddy to so many people, that cruddy came back on them.

"Why you leave your brother on the cement, watch him having trouble with his breathing. Die for no reason, niggas be dying for no reason."

He wasn't no **Usual Suspect**, and I'm not **Keyser Soze**, but I pieced the murder together. From the clues that homicide gave me, to the lady story, it all added up. His cousin killed him, his brother left him for dead while running his pockets and leaving him gasping for air while running across the street hiding his belongings in the closet.

Truiee died for no reason, but deeper than that in the end, Truiee knew and carried out his purpose. Truiee music told his story, and his music will forever be a part of history. One thing you don't get back in the end is time. In the 22 years he had on this earth, he used his time to serve his purpose, so in the end he left a lifelong Legacy.

"Yo , a lot of niggas out here lose they self, and forget who they are, because of the niggas that they hang around yo, always remember yo, keep your same personality, Don't ever change your character. Just stay 100 man."

Truiee

No matter who he was around, he was himself. He made it cool to still be a civilian, which was a term meaning non-gang related, and manifest who you are and what you have to offer this earth.

Three days before his murder he made a song about the bad energy he was feeling around him. He felt it. It's like he was getting prepared. One step away from success, after all the balled up pieces of paper in his book bag, to making music in the basement with his best friend, he had just got reconnected with the music plug he awaited all his life, and he gets killed. Moments become memories, and memories become history.

Seven chapters in this book, because seven (7) is the number of completion. Each chapter named after his songs because his music tells his story. Truiee was 11 when I birthed his baby brother Chayce, and Chayce was 11 when I buried Truiee. 1124 is his birthday (14) and my birthday (21) combined, so on the days we were both born into this world, he left.

On 1124 he didn't die, the soul never dies, he went to a higher form of life as he transitioned into a LeGend. True story, about Truiee, 1124, IT WAS ALREADY WRITTEN.

CPSIA information can be obtained
at www.ICGtesting.com
Printed in the USA
LVHW071206250223
740353LV00010B/478

9 781685 158354